TEEN LIFE™

FREQUENTLY ASKED QUESTIONS ABOUT

Texting, Sexting, and Flaming

Rebecca T. Klein

ROSEN
PUBLISHING®
New York

Published in 2013 by The Rosen Publishing Group, Inc.
29 East 21st Street, New York, NY 10010

Library of Congress Cataloging-in-Publication Data

Klein, Rebecca T.
Frequently asked questions about texting, sexting, and
flaming/Rebecca T. Klein.—1st ed.
    p. cm.—(FAQ: teen life)
Includes bibliographical references and index.
ISBN 978-1-4488-8331-8 (library binding)
1. Internet and teenagers—Juvenile literature. 2. Text
messages (Cell phone systems)—Juvenile literature. 3.
Sexting—Juvenile literature. 4. Online etiquette—Juvenile
literature. 5. Interpersonal communication—Juvenile
literature. I. Title.
HQ799.2.I5K52 2013
302.23'1—dc23

                                                    2012018902

Manufactured in the United States of America

CPSIA Compliance Information: Batch #W13YA: For further information, contact Rosen Publishing, New York, New York,
at 1-800-237-9932.

Contents

one

HOW HAS TEXTING CHANGED THE WAY WE COMMUNICATE?

Texting has completely changed the way that we communicate with each other. People of all ages have begun to text one another as often as, if not more often than, they call each other. The Wireless Trade Association conducted a survey in which youth ages fourteen to nineteen claimed that they spend equal amounts of time talking and texting. Many of the youth interviewed (54 percent of the girls and 40 percent of the boys) said that their social lives "would end or be worsened" if they did not text. Texting has changed our culture in positive ways and in negative ways. Let's look at why we text so much, how it affects us, and how we can use texting in a responsible manner.

Why We Text

Texting can definitely be more convenient than making a phone call. If you have a small piece of information to

Texting has become a huge part of youth culture. Research by the Wireless Trade Association shows that teenagers spend as much time texting as they spend talking.

communicate—such as the time and place of a meeting—a text can be a good way to pass that information along. Sometimes you may not have time for a full conversation, or you may be in an area that does not have good cell phone reception. Other times, you may be in a situation where an actual phone conversation would be disruptive. When the purpose of communication is to pass along simple information, texting can be a great tool.

However, if the nature of the communication is more complicated or deals with matters of emotion, texting is generally a bad idea. It can be very tempting to text in these situations, since important conversations are sometimes scary. Some people also feel that they communicate better through writing than they do out loud. But there are a lot of potential problems with using text messages to convey important emotional issues.

When Should I Not Text?

Let's say that you are in a fight with a close friend. You haven't spoken to each other in a week, and every time you see the friend, you avoid making eye contact. You want to make up with your friend, or at least get some closure to the situation. You may be afraid of his or her reaction. You may worry that you will be rejected if you reach out. It is extremely tempting to send a text message, rather than making a phone call or confronting your friend in person. However, there are many potential problems with handling the situation that way.

For some people, a text message seems less personal than a phone call. But even if everyone agrees (as many kids these days do) that texting is an appropriate way to have important conversations, it presents some problems. Many people use emoticons (smiley faces, frowning faces, etc.) to signify their mood when sending a text or talking online. But no matter how many emoticons you use, you can never convey the same emotion through text that you would be able to show face-to-face. You may make a comment that you mean sincerely, and your friend may interpret it as sarcastic. Or your

Although it can be tempting to use texting to avoid having uncomfortable conversations in person, this can lead to a lot of miscommunication. It is wiser to have important conversations face-to-face.

friend may say something playfully and forget to include the smiley face, and you will think he or she is serious. Before you know it, the text message conversation has turned into another set of problems, rather than making things better, as you intended. Important conversations should always be handled in person, or at least through a phone call. If the idea of initiating the conversation out of the blue is too scary, you might send a text message asking the person if he or she is willing to get together and talk. But the actual talk should definitely occur face-to-face.

Another potential pitfall of texting is that it can distract you from your surroundings. Sending a quick text to communicate useful information during a study session at the library is fine. But if the conversation goes on too long, you might lose focus on your studies. This is also true of texting during class. In order to avoid distraction, you should keep your phone off or tucked away in your pocket or backpack during class. Any messages you may get during this time will be waiting when you are finished.

It is also a good idea to stay off of your phone when you're traveling from one place to another. We have all been in a situation where we're walking down the street and the person in front of us stops suddenly or the person next to us veers into us. More often than not, that person has a cell phone in his or her hand. Don't be that person. Usually, any texting you need to do can wait until you reach your destination. If you absolutely must text while you are walking somewhere, step over to the side so that you are not blocking foot traffic.

Texting While Driving

Speaking of traffic, you should never, ever text while you are driving. When you disrupt foot traffic, it is usually just annoying and not dangerous. But when you're in a car, it becomes a matter of safety—sometimes even of life and death. According to the Don't Text and Drive Web site, a 2007 study revealed that 46 percent of teens admit to texting while driving. The same study also found that texting was just as likely as drinking to inhibit a teen's ability to drive safely.

Texting while driving has played a part in many fatal automobile crashes. In Brooklyn, New York, in 2010, teenage

Texting while driving distracts you from the road and puts you, your passengers, and other drivers in danger. No matter how important the message is, it can wait until you are safely off the road.

driver Nechama Rothberger crashed into the truck of delivery-eryman Tian Sheng Lin. The crash rendered him brain-dead, and he later passed away. In their investigation, police discovered a half-written text message on the girl's phone at the time of the crash.

Because of incidents like this one, many states have declared it illegal to text or talk on the phone while driving. To avoid harming yourself, your passengers, and other drivers, keep your phone off or out of reach while you are driving. No message is important enough to jeopardize your safety or the safety of others.

Another, though milder, danger of text messaging is tenosynovitis, a condition that is also referred to as "text messenger's thumb." This is a real medical condition, caused by excessive texting. The symptoms are pain and tenderness of the thumb, and if untreated, it can become chronic. The phone company Virgin Mobile has a Web site that gives examples of "texter-cises," which are hand exercises designed to keep the frequent texter's hand in decent shape.

Texting, Internet Communication, and School Performance

You may hear a lot of talk from adults about how cell phones and the Internet distract kids from their studies. People who grew up without all this technology at their fingertips are often quick to point out the negative aspects. But in doing so, they forget to examine the positive effects of constant written verbal communication. If you approach it the right way, the writing you do online and through text messages can help you become a better writer all around, including in school. Blog posts, e-mails, and even text messages can help you practice writing.

Of course, there are going to be differences between the writing that you do for school and the casual conversations that you have with your friends over text or instant messaging. Just as many of us speak differently with our friends than we would speak to a teacher or in a job interview, the language that we use over text or in IMs differs from the language we use for academic writing. In casual communication, we use slang and often follow different grammatical rules than the ones we need to follow in formal English. When this casual communication happens over text or IM, we use all sorts of abbreviations. You probably type the terms "btw," "j/k," and "lol" on a daily basis. You probably have countless other abbreviations and codes that help you communicate quickly with your friends. You may even develop your own terms that no one outside of your circle understands. Slang terms and abbreviations are fine in casual situations where everyone understands them and has agreed that it is OK to use them. However, when you are writing for school, you need to switch into a different mode of thinking and follow the universally accepted rules of the English language. This doesn't mean that the way you speak and write with your friends is bad or wrong. But knowing the difference, and knowing how to follow the rules of proper English when necessary, will be an incredible help to you in school and in your professional life.

Practicing Writing Through Electronic Communications

There are many ways that you can practice aspects of academic writing in your text messages and other electronic communications. Even when you use slang terms and abbreviations, you can make an effort to use proper punctuation and structure your sentences correctly. You can also practice synonyms, trying to come up with different ways to say the same thing. Texting is also a great way to practice concision (making yourself fully understood using as few words as possible). Some cell phones force you to do this by having a limit on the number of characters you can type in one message. And even if your phone doesn't have this limit, your thumbs probably get tired after long periods of texting. Instead of relying only on abbreviations to shorten your messages, try thinking of different, shorter ways to say what you need to say. Developing this skill will make your academic writing cleaner and stronger.

The Benefits of Being a "Digital Native"

People your age and younger, who have grown up in a digital world, are sometimes referred to as "digital natives," while people who made the transition from a pre-Internet world are called "digital immigrants." You often hear digital immigrants saying that the Internet and other forms of technology have made today's kids lazy and shortened their attention spans. Adults often look at a kid who is listening to music on headphones while writing a paper on a laptop and texting a friend at the same time, and wonder how the kid can possibly be focused on any of the tasks at hand. But not all adults see things this way. In his article "Growing Up Digital," John Seely Brown points out how the attention spans of today's kids mirror those of top managers in the corporate world, indicating that multitasking will be useful to many students in their future careers. Seely Brown talks about how the Internet has changed the meaning of "literacy." In the past, literacy simply meant the ability to read and write. This form of literacy (which Seely Brown attributes to the technology of the typewriter) is narrow in that it acknowledges only one type of intelligence. The Web has created a new kind of literacy that incorporates many different types of intelligence. Of course, the Web uses words, but it also uses visual, musical, and kinesthetic (physical) elements, to name a few. To be Web savvy, people must practice skills beyond simply being able to read and write. They must be able to sift through the vast amounts of information and entertainment available on the Web to find the things they need. They must be navigators. Seely Brown also talks about how the Web can create a "community of learners," allowing people to benefit from and build upon each other's knowledge. Many teachers are catching onto the benefits of using the Internet in the classroom. There are even social networking sites that are specifically designed to be used in schools. Students can post questions and submit assignments through these sites and have a central space to interact with their teacher and their classmates outside of school hours. Imagine that you've forgotten what your teacher assigned for homework or that you don't understand part of the assignment. You could just post your question on the class social networking site and quickly get a response from one of your classmates or even directly from your teacher. There are countless ways that digital communication can be helpful for today's students.

two

WHAT SHOULD I KNOW ABOUT SEXTING?

"Sexting" is a fairly new word. The term did not even exist a few years ago, but it is used often in the media these days. The word is a combination of the words "sex" and "texting." It refers to the exchange, over the phone, of sexually explicit text messages or photos. The media often suggest that the practice of sexting is widespread among teenagers and middle schoolers. According to the Federal Bureau of Investigation (FBI), 20 percent of teenagers have sent images of themselves partially clothed or fully nude to someone else over the phone or have posted these images online. Twenty percent may not sound like a lot, but that statistic doesn't account for those kids who are sending sexual text messages without photos. Even considering only the 20 percent who send photos, sexting is definitely

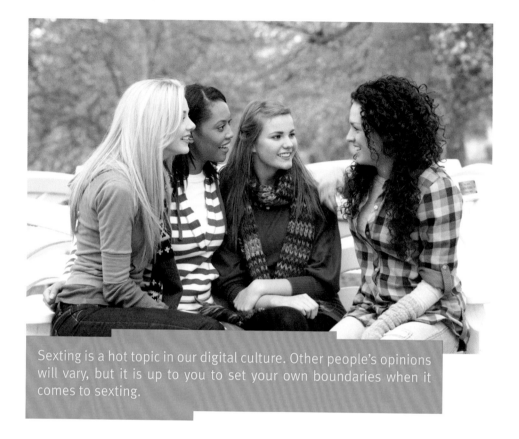

Sexting is a hot topic in our digital culture. Other people's opinions will vary, but it is up to you to set your own boundaries when it comes to sexting.

something that you should be aware of and be prepared to deal with if you are confronted by it.

When Texting Becomes Sexting

You might not always be sure where the line is between normal text messaging and sexting. You may talk about sex with your friends and jokingly exchange messages that could be interpreted as explicit, but you wouldn't define these messages as sexting. However, if you are texting with someone about sexual things that you might, either hypothetically or in reality, do with him or her, that would definitely be sexting. Any time you send or receive suggestive pictures also qualifies.

There are a lot of things to consider when you are deciding whether or not to engage in this type of text messaging. Your parents, friends, teachers, and religious leaders would all have advice to give you, and they might all tell you different things, but the ultimate decision is your own. First of all, you need to figure out whether you are comfortable with the things that are being said to you and the things that you are saying. You are the only person who can decide that. One way to gauge your level of comfort is to think about whether or not you would be willing to say the same things face-to-face. If the person you are sexting with brought up your conversation in person the next day, how would you feel about it? If you could discuss it openly or joke about it, then you may be comfortable. But if you would be mortified, you may need to think twice about having that type of conversation, even over text. You should absolutely never send any pictures that make you uncomfortable, no matter how much anyone pressures you. And if you are the one requesting racy pictures or explicit conversations, you should be incredibly considerate of the other person's boundaries.

With photos, there are legal concerns to consider as well. You probably know that it is illegal on both a state and federal level for adults to possess or distribute child pornography. But did you know that it is illegal for minors to possess or distribute explicit images of other minors? And the law even goes one step further: it is also illegal for minors to distribute explicit photos of themselves. So if you send a nude photo to your boyfriend or girlfriend, you could be putting both of you at risk of doing jail time and becoming registered sex offenders. This may sound ridiculous, and you may feel that you have the right to send pictures of yourself if you want to. And obviously, sending a picture of yourself to your boyfriend or girlfriend is not the same thing as distributing child porn. But in many cases these laws were written before cell phones and sexting existed. Although some people are working to change the laws so that they would treat sexting differently, the legal system has not yet caught up with the technology. Also, even if you intend for your boyfriend, girlfriend, or crush to be the only recipient of the photo, it could reach the eyes of many unintended recipients, including adults and young children. One junior high student in upstate New York sent a photo of himself to a classmate, and she forwarded it to friends who forwarded it to their friends. Eventually, more than three hundred kids saw the picture. Would you want three hundred people to see an explicit photo of you?

There is already a history of youth who have engaged in sexting being prosecuted for felony pandering obscenities and child pornography charges. While some people are working to change the laws that allow for this, others feel that kids who originate and distribute explicit photos should be punished as harshly as adults. The laws vary from state to state, and the punishments vary from judge to judge. Keep these facts in mind when you are deciding what type of pictures you want to send to other people or have them send to you.

No matter how much you feel that you can trust someone, if you decide to engage in sexting with that person, it is essential to protect your boundaries and your privacy.

Protecting Your Boundaries

If you do decide to sext with someone, it is important to be clear about your intentions and to know what the other person's intentions are. You need to be clear about whether what you are saying is hypothetical or if you intend to follow through on any of it. This can help lessen the risk of awkward or dangerous situations occurring in person. And remember that you should not let anyone pressure you into doing things that you're not ready for, regardless of what you have said over text message. Even if you weren't clear that the sexting was all in fun, you have the right, and the responsibility, to set physical boundaries if something makes you uncomfortable. And if you are the one who wants to make the sexting into a reality, you have a responsibility to respect your partner's wishes and boundaries. Even if your partner has been forward or explicit over text messages, he or she is not obligated to do anything physically.

Privacy is a concern in this situation as well, especially regarding the pictures. Before sending anything explicit, words or pictures, you should think very hard about the level of trust you have with the person you are sending them to. The last thing you want is for your pictures to be plastered in a bathroom or shared on the Internet. It would also be embarrassing to have your text messages read aloud to a group of friends for entertainment purposes. Both girls and boys can be vicious when it comes to this type of thing. Before you send anything, make sure you think about all of the eyes that could possibly see it. You may think that you can trust the person you are sexting with anything. But what happens if you have a fight? The picture could be distributed to the person's friends or posted on the Internet. This would not only be embarrassing, but it would also increase the risk of the photo reaching legal authorities. The person who originated the image (you) could face jail time and sex offender status. Is sending that photo really worth the risk?

It's easy to forget a lot of these things in the moment. Because text messages are typed, rather than spoken aloud, it's easy to think of them as a game. You may start saying things that you normally wouldn't, just to see what kind of reaction you get from the other person. Sexting can provide a thrill, and you probably feel that it is safer and less scary than doing something physical with the person you like. There is some truth to that. Obviously, sexting with someone is not the same as having physical sex. The risks and concerns are different, but they are still risks. You need to protect yourself, just as you would if engaging in actual sex. Sexting is a form of intimacy, too, and it requires a strong level of trust. And it cannot be stressed enough how careful you should be about sending or receiving any kind of explicit photos.

Myths and Facts

Minors can't get in trouble for sending or possessing inappropriate pictures of themselves or of other minors.

Fact: ➡ They absolutely can. It is illegal for anyone to possess or distribute pornographic images of a minor, regardless of the age of the perpetrator. You can be legally prosecuted for doing so, even if the pictures you send are of yourself. People convicted on child pornography charges often face extremely strict sentences, including long stretches of jail time and the requirement that they register as sex offenders when they leave jail. The law makes no exception for minors on these charges, nor does it require any leniency in the sentencing of a convicted minor.

If I erase a text message, there is no record of it.

Fact: ➡ Even if you have erased a text message from your phone, or never sent it in the first place, the phone's memory still holds a record of everything you have typed. With the right technology, it could be recovered. Also, your phone company may have a record of all of your messages, regardless of whether or not they are saved in your phone. While it is difficult to retrieve an erased text message, and it is generally only attempted by forensic specialists, it is definitely possible.

I can't get in trouble for harassing someone on the Internet or through text messages. As long as I don't touch the person, they're just words, and words can't hurt.

Fact: ●➤ Words can have just as much of a negative effect on a person as physical pain can—sometimes even more. Research has shown that the same two parts of the brain, the anterior cingulated cortex and the right ventral prefrontal cortex, are active when social rejection occurs and when physical pain is inflicted. This suggests that social exclusion, even online, can create similar trauma to physical abuse; names *can* hurt, sometimes as much as sticks and stones. Many states are beginning to develop antibullying laws, which make verbal harassment a crime just like physical assault.

three

WHAT IS FLAMING AND WHY DO PEOPLE DO IT?

The word "flaming" is used to describe hostile interaction on the Internet. It includes mean posts on message boards, angry comments on news Web sites, or e-mails full of insults. When this type of hostility occurs between people who know one another, it is often referred to as cyberbullying. Cyberbullying involves malicious posts directed at a classmate, acquaintance, or friend, and it is usually intended to be seen by others in that person's social circle. For example, if someone uses the Internet to spread a rumor that a classmate cheated on his or her boyfriend or girlfriend or posts a mortifying picture of a friend, that would be cyberbullying. In extreme cases, entire Web sites have been created for the purpose of ridiculing someone. This type of bullying often has serious emotional and psychological effects on the victim, and it can have serious legal consequences for the bullies.

On the Internet, just like in real-life social situations, people get into arguments and debates, and sometimes they gang up on each other or say hurtful things to one another.

However, not all arguments on the Internet are that malicious or calculated.

Flaming is a broader term, including arguments with strangers. Sometimes people get into debates on the Internet about topics like religion, politics, race, or sexual orientation. Many times, these debates turn into arguments, and they end up becoming personal. Soon, the people involved have forgotten all about the topic they were discussing in the beginning. Instead, they begin insulting each other's grammar, picking each other's posts apart, and even digging up personal information about each other to fuel their attacks. When one of these arguments goes on for a long time, or other people are drawn into the fight, it becomes a flame war.

Trolling

The idea of strangers arguing with each other online might seem silly to you. You may feel that you'd never waste your time getting involved in a flame war. However, there are some people online who make it a point to draw their fellow Internet users into flame wars. They go into forums or chat rooms simply for the purpose of starting arguments. On the Internet, these people are referred to as "trolls."

In fairy tales and other folklore, a troll is a scary, inhuman being that hides under bridges to scare people. On the Internet, a troll hides or lurks in a chat room or a forum, waiting to pounce on other users. Often the troll doesn't contribute anything of value to the discussion. He or she simply looks for opportunities to stir up trouble, making offensive comments about the subject matter or about other users. There are a few different reasons why someone might engage in trolling.

The simplest explanation for trolling is boredom. Just as people pick arguments with their friends or siblings when they can't think of anything else to do, some people choose to pick arguments on the Internet.

Experienced Internet users will often caution others to avoid "feeding the troll." What they mean is, don't encourage the troll or add any more fuel for his or her argument. If no one argues back, the troll is likely to become bored with the very argument he or she started.

Another reason why people might start an online argument is to prove that they have superior knowledge of a particular subject. These people may hunt around on the Internet for forums or posts that deal with a subject on which they consider themselves an expert. Then they challenge anyone else who displays knowledge, trying to contradict or one-up the other person's comments. If they can't find any fault with the ideas expressed in the post, they will point out incorrect grammar, typos, or misspelled words, or go for petty tactics like making fun of other people's usernames.

Whatever the specific reason or method, insecurity plays a large role in flaming and trolling. Often people who are insecure in physical social settings find an opportunity to be outgoing on the Internet. They feel safer behind the protective barrier of a computer screen or a keyboard. From behind that buffer, they display aggression that they would never show toward people in a face-to-face argument. Another slang term that has developed for this type of Internet pseudo-toughness is "e-thugging." When a group of students was interviewed about this phenomenon, one of them said that being mean was easier on the Internet because, "When you are on the computer, you don't have to see the hurt in their eyes." The same interview revealed that students felt more comfortable swearing online and saying all kinds of things that they would never say to someone face-to-face. The good news, however, is that many of them also felt more comfortable confronting people about

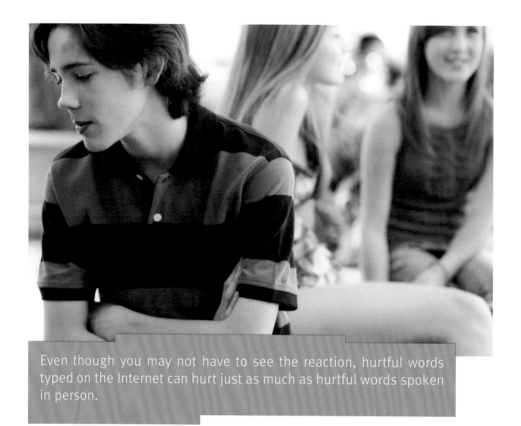

Even though you may not have to see the reaction, hurtful words typed on the Internet can hurt just as much as hurtful words spoken in person.

online harassment through the Internet. They mentioned that it is much easier to type "Knock it off" than it is to say something that aggressive face-to-face.

It is also a good idea to be on the lookout for trolls who may bait you for personal information, such as credit card numbers, phone numbers, or your home address. This type of trolling is sometimes easy to spot; the posts look like obvious bait for scams. But trolls get very creative and may embed false or dangerous URLs in a post that looks normal. They may even use an argument to coax you into visiting a Web site. Never click on a link that you can't be sure is trustworthy. You could infect your computer with a virus that could harm your operating system or install spyware, which could extract personal information from your computer and browsing history.

Flame Wars and Social Networking

Trolls tend to frequent forums and the comment sections of news sites and often interact anonymously. However, flame wars are also common on social networking sites. In these cases, the fight usually starts in the comment thread of a post or a status update.

It can be embarrassing and uncomfortable when a flame war starts over one of your comments or status updates. The best way to try and shut it down is to stop participating.

It may involve the person who actually made the post, but often it occurs between two or more of that user's "friends." They may disagree about the content of the post. What begins as a debate can quickly devolve into a mess of name-calling and vicious insults.

This is unpleasant for anyone who reads the thread, and, as you know if you have ever had this happen on a post of yours, it is embarrassing and uncomfortable for the person who made the initial post. It can feel sort of like you hosted a party and two of your guests got into a fight. Even though you may have had no part in sparking the argument, you feel responsible to mediate it. A social networking site is sort of like a party. People with very different backgrounds and beliefs interact with one another through mutual friends and interests. This is one of the coolest things about social networking, but it also means that arguments can spring up frequently and unexpectedly.

Preventing Flame Wars

Even if we know better and realize that flaming is silly, most people who use the Internet will eventually find themselves wrapped up in some kind of debate. When it remains healthy, Internet debating is a great way to learn and practice how to clearly communicate your ideas. But the trick is to make sure that your debate stays a debate and does not become a flame war. There are a few things you can keep in mind to help you do this.

Remember that while you cannot control what other people say, you can definitely control your own words. Choose them wisely. When you participate in Internet discussions, stay on topic; try not to veer off into personal territory or insults. When you disagree with a point that someone else has made, politely explain your own opinion, without attacking the person with whom you disagree. Even if you find that person's opinion offensive, you can maintain a level of respect for the person in the way that you express that. This level of respect not only helps prevent flame wars, but it also increases the possibility that the other person will take your point into serious consideration. If you resort to insults, however, that is all the other person will notice, and your point will be lost.

Sometimes, no matter how polite you are, another person will seem determined to turn the debate into a flame war. In this situation, remember that an argument requires two participants. If you refuse to respond to personal insults and rude comments, the other person will probably lose interest. He or she can't argue if no one argues back. If you have a hard time reading the person's comments without responding, it might be a good idea to remove yourself from the discussion thread altogether. Just as a fire will die without oxygen, a flame war will be extinguished if it is given no fuel.

four

CAN I GET IN TROUBLE FOR MY PRIVATE MESSAGES, POSTS, AND TEXTS?

There are all kinds of things that you say to your friends that you would never say to your parents, your teachers, or the general public. As discussed earlier, we have different modes of communication in different settings. This applies not only to the way we speak, but also to the content of that speech—that is, the actual meaning of what we say. We share secrets with our friends and discuss matters candidly that we might think twice about discussing with strangers. When that communication happens in person, you can be reasonably sure that it won't fall upon the wrong ears, especially if you know your friends to be trustworthy. But when you are communicating over the Internet or through text message, you need to reexamine the idea of a "private" conversation.

When we share secrets with our friends, we trust that they will keep our secrets safe. But when you post a secret online, it is much harder to protect your privacy.

The nature of privacy is especially precarious on social networking sites. Often the default settings leave all of your posts open to the public. This means that if you don't change the settings, anyone can pull up your profile and read what is posted there. You can change the settings to limit who can see your profile, but oftentimes you have to do this for each specific kind of post. Your friends' privacy settings also affect who can see what they post on your profile and what you post on theirs. And even if everyone has everything set up so that only friends can see their posts, privacy is not guaranteed. Think about how many times people read over your shoulder while you are online or how often you forget to log out before getting up from a computer, leaving your profile wide open to the next person who sits down. None of this should make you paranoid, but it should make you mindful of the things you are posting.

In addition to questionable privacy settings, you should also be aware of technology that allows parents, teachers, or employers to monitor your computer usage. Oftentimes parents, schools, or workplaces install programs that block the user of a computer from accessing certain sites. These systems function on either an "allow" list, which allows access only to approved sites, or a "deny" list, which blacklists certain sites. Some of these filters can screen the e-mails, chats, and posts that you send while you are using the computer. Sometimes, however, they go a step further and install software that traces the browsing history or allows remote monitoring of a specific computer. If remote monitoring is installed, this means that at any point in time, from another computer, someone else is able to view exactly what appears on your screen.

There is some dissent regarding the use of restrictive software by schools to monitor students' Internet usage. In the book *School Policies*, from the Opposing Viewpoints series published by the Gale Group, some of the essays denounce this software as violating students' privacy and promoting censorship. In his essay "School Surveillance Technology Is Totalitarian," Ronnie Casella argues that this technology is promoted by the government and by security companies to promote their own agendas, particularly financial gain. Others in the same book argue that

Schools and libraries often install monitoring software. These precautions can protect you from online predators, but they can also be used to track your Internet usage.

the technology is good and necessary because it protects kids from online predators. Whatever you feel about the technology, it is a wise idea to be familiar with the policies that apply to any computer you are using and to know what kind of monitoring software is installed. Make sure that you read the policies put forth by your school, library, or any other public location where you are using the Internet.

Text messages are a bit more private, but technology exists to monitor those, too. Your phone company will have a record of the text messages that you have sent and received. And if you ever watch cop shows, you are probably familiar with the concept of a cell phone "dump," a procedure that reveals the phone's call and text message history. There are two types of cell phone dumps: a "logical" dump, which extracts some of the information from the phone's memory, and a "physical" dump, which copies the entire flash memory of the phone. A physical dump may even reveal text messages that were typed but never sent, since the phone's memory records each keystroke; your phone remembers every time you press a button! Cell phone dump procedures are generally used only by forensic experts in criminal cases, but it is a good idea to be aware of all the possibilities for revealing your "private" messages. Also keep in mind that if you leave your phone laying around and unlocked, anyone can access your text history.

Why Privacy Matters

You may be wondering why privacy is such a big deal. If you are not engaging in anything illegal or malicious, you may not feel as though you need to protect your communication from outside viewers. And to some extent, this may be true. However, there are many factors to consider.

Sometimes kids post things on the Internet that they intend in a playful or joking manner, and subsequent events paint those things in a malicious light. And sometimes kids deliberately taunt and harass their classmates and peers. In recent years, there has been a rash of teenagers committing suicide due to excessive bullying, much of which has taken place online. In

Tyler Clementi committed suicide after being bullied online. Many states have begun to implement laws against cyberbullying. Clementi's roommate, Dharun Ravi, was convicted of using a webcam to spy on Clementi in 2012.

South Hadley, Massachusetts, in 2010, fifteen-year-old Phoebe Prince killed herself after being harassed on Facebook and Twitter because she had dated a popular senior. That same year, eighteen-year-old Rutgers student Tyler Clementi committed suicide after his roommate had used a webcam to watch him engaging sexually with a man and had posted about it on Twitter. In both cases, legal action was pursued against the teens who posted the material in question.

In response to these and similar events, many states have implemented laws that make cyberbullying an offense that can be prosecuted in court. More than thirty states have amended the language of their harassment laws to include cyberbullying. In late 2011, New York senator Jeffrey Klein introduced a bill that would make cyberbullying itself a misdemeanor. The legislation also addresses "bullycide," which it defines as suicide intentionally brought on by cyberbullying. The bill would allow bullycide to be prosecuted as second-degree manslaughter, a class C felony. Hopefully, you would think twice about posting anything that could be hurtful or insulting to someone else, regardless of the possible negative effects it could have on you. However, it is also wise to keep your own interests in mind and protect yourself from legal consequences.

Another thing to be aware of is the concept of your "Internet footprint." Think of this as the image of you that someone would gather from looking at your Internet usage. To get an idea of what this might look like, try plugging your name into a search engine and looking at what comes up. This is exactly what many employers do when they are scanning through résumés and job applications. If the first thing that comes up is a picture of you chugging beer at a party or holding up your middle finger, you may want to consider making some changes to the things you post online. There is nothing wrong with being goofy or taking pictures of the fun you have with your friends. But more and more, the first impressions that employers or even future significant others have of us come from the Internet. Who knows, college admissions departments may even look at your profile. Many of the things that you post on the Internet are visible to the entire world.

It is important to consider your future when posting things that will become part of your Internet footprint. Future employers may conduct searches to look at your posts and photos.

You want to be sure that you present yourself in the most positive light that you can.

We mentioned earlier that some trolls go after your personal information online. This is another reason to be conscientious about privacy when using the Internet. Many public networks are unsecured, which means that with the right technology, someone could gain access to your passwords and other information while you are using the network. You can help to lessen this possibility by making sure that you log out of all accounts when you are finished using them, and close your browser altogether when you are done.

Ten Great Questions to Ask Yourself Before You Send a Text Message or Post

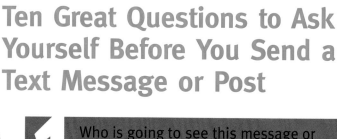

1 Who is going to see this message or image? Will it reach more than its intended audience?

2 How does this post make me look? Does it portray me in a positive light?

3 Could this post or text message get me in trouble, either legally or otherwise?

4 Could this message or post be hurtful to someone else?

5 Is this a conversation or piece of information that should be shared privately?

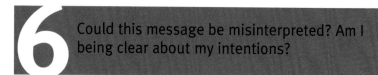

6 Could this message be misinterpreted? Am I being clear about my intentions?

7 Is this a conversation that would be more productive in person?

8 After I send this message or post, will I be embarrassed to see the person to whom I sent it?

9 How would I feel if I received this type of message in my in-box or on my profile?

10 Can I trust that the person to whom I'm sending this will respect my privacy?

five

HOW CAN I HELP STOP ELECTRONIC HARASSMENT?

So far we have talked mostly about protecting your own privacy and regulating your own activity online and over text messages. Controlling and taking responsibility for the things you post or text is fairly straightforward. It requires some discipline and self-awareness, but it is definitely in your realm of control. It may be much harder, however, to predict or control the things that other people say to you. If you or someone you care about is dealing with harassment, either online or through text messages, you may be confused about what you can do to stop it. Here are some tips for dealing with specific instances of harassment and for helping to eradicate the problem in general. Remember that if you feel overwhelmed or have any fear that you are in physical danger, you should seek the help of an adult that you trust. Electronic harassment, or cyberstalking, is

It is important to talk to a parent or a trusted adult if you are a victim of continued harassment or if you know someone who is being harassed.

against the law. If the person refuses to stop when asked, there are further legal steps you can take. An adult can help you through that process.

What to Do If Someone Is Harassing You

If you are receiving messages that make you angry or uncomfortable, you have every right to protect yourself by stopping them. No matter how the exchange began, or how much you have participated, you have the right to preserve your dignity

Set clear boundaries regarding texting or online communication. If someone refuses to respect those boundaries, stop the communication and seek the help of an adult.

and set boundaries. There are a few different types of situations in which you may need to exercise this right.

Let's say you are engaged in a text message conversation with someone that you have a crush on. The conversation begins with some light flirtation and escalates to a point where both of you start to say some racy things. But at this point, your crush has started to make you uncomfortable by asking for nude photos or sending messages that are more explicit than you intended. As soon as this line is crossed, let the person know that you are uncomfortable with the current territory of the conversation. You could even try doing this jokingly, saying something like "Slow down there, killer," or "Let's back this up a bit." If that doesn't get the point across, you may need to be more direct. Tell the person that you were enjoying the conversation at first, but now it is making you uncomfortable. If he or she is asking for nude pictures, say that it would technically be illegal for you to send one. While you're at it, warn the person that he or she could get in trouble for sending and receiving these photos, too. If the person continues to press the issue, you should stop responding. If you continue to receive messages after you have removed yourself from the conversation, you may need to explore the possibility of blocking the person. You might be able to do this automatically through your phone or you might need to contact your phone company. If you need help figuring out how to block someone, or if you feel that your safety is in danger, speak to a trusted adult right away. Excessive text messaging is covered under cyberstalking laws.

You might also find yourself in difficult situations online. Maybe you've had an argument with a friend, and she has taken to the Internet to vent anger. She has started posting insults on your profile or publicly posted an embarrassing photo of you that she had previously sworn to hide forever. Or maybe the person is a complete stranger who disagrees with a comment you made on someone else's status or on a public Web forum. Your first priority is to get the offensive material offline. Usually, if someone has posted something on your profile, you will have the option to remove it. If you do not have the capacity to remove the post, politely demand that the person remove it himself or herself. Then request that he or she stop harassing you. You will probably be tempted to retaliate in some way against the things that were said or done, but you need to resist that desire. Retaliation will only escalate and prolong the argument. Again, if the person refuses to comply with your request to stop, speak with a teacher or a parent about further action you can take to end the harassment.

If a classmate or a friend is being harassed, sometimes the best thing you can do is to show your friend a supportive face. Refusing to participate in the harassment is a brave step in itself, but you can go one step further and stick up for the person who is being harassed. As we mentioned earlier, it is just as easy to

If you know someone who is being harassed online or through text messages, offer your support and stick up for that person. Just one friendly face can make a huge difference.

stand up to a bully over the Internet as it is to *be* a bully over the Internet. You could send the bully a message, either publicly or privately, letting him or her know that you disagree with the comments. However, defending someone who is being picked on doesn't require entering into the discussion if you are uncomfortable with that. You can simply be friendly toward the person who is being victimized. This will help that person feel supported and will silently show the harassers that you disagree with their actions.

You can also set an example by refusing to participate in flaming and cyber or text harassment. If people try to draw you into this type of behavior, tell them that you have better things to do with your time. If they press you or ask you why you won't participate, tell them why you are against these practices. Explain that you find them hurtful and unnecessary, and that harassing someone from behind a cell phone or a computer screen doesn't make them tough. If your friends still insist, you cannot control their behavior, but you can refrain from laughing or egging them on. Lots of times, people are motivated by a need for attention. If you do not give them that attention, they may lose interest and stop what they're doing. If they realize that other people are not impressed by their cyber toughness, there will be no reason to continue.

Further Action

Even if you are not personally being harassed and do not know anyone else who is, you might be interested in helping

If you want to fight cyberharassment at your school, get together with other committed classmates and adults, and organize a club to raise awareness.

to prevent cyberharassment and cyberbullying. Just because the problem isn't currently affecting you, that doesn't mean that you can't be concerned. There are several things that you can do to help protect yourself, your friends, and others. If you feel especially passionate about ending harassment and bullying, either online or elsewhere, you might consider taking on a leadership role in your school. You could start an antibullying club or an Internet safety awareness club. You could also find out what policies, if any, your school has developed around the issue of bullying, Internet safety, cell phone usage, etc. If there aren't any, or if you disagree with the existing policies, encourage change by starting a petition or speaking at a student council or school board meeting. If this issue is important to you, reach out to organizations that are committed to making the Internet a safer and friendlier place. They have information and resources that can help you explore the cause and educate others.

And, as we've mentioned, teach by example. Make sure that you have your important conversations in person. Bullying, harassment, and arguments of all kinds develop and thrive when both parties can hide behind computer screens or cell phones. Electronic communication is the norm these days. By using it primarily for the exchange of information and refraining from having important and emotional conversations through electronic means, you can help make sure that the positive aspects of electronic communication thrive and that the negative aspects die out.

In order to protect yourself, learn the laws governing electronic communication, and become intimately familiar with the privacy settings of any sites, like Facebook, that you use.

You should also become as familiar as possible with the laws and policies that govern electronic communication. Learn about the privacy features of all your social networking sites and the monitoring devices used by your school and library. Be aware of the child pornography laws mentioned, as well as the cyberstalking and cyberbullying laws for your state. Knowing these things not only helps you protect yourself from doing anything that could cause legal ramifications, but also helps you learn your own rights if someone is harassing you.

The advent of cell phones and the Internet has completely revolutionized our culture. These tools have made communication possible on a much larger scale and have connected us to people all around the world. They have opened up countless possibilities and allowed us to become and remain friends with people regardless of their distance from us. We are now used to being able to communicate all the time, with people we know and with people we have never met. Texting, sexting, and flaming are all products of these relatively new technologies. Adults are still learning about these phenomena, and our laws and research are still catching up. But as a teenager who encounters these things in everyday life, you know the importance of being informed and making wise decisions. When it comes to communication, electronic or otherwise, it often comes down to simply respecting yourself and the other people involved. Respect yourself enough to set boundaries and protect your privacy, and respect others enough to honor theirs. Be empathetic. Put yourself in the other person's place and think about how he or she feels. If we all did that, then most of the laws wouldn't even be necessary.

Glossary

blocking A service offered by some cell phone companies and Internet sites in which you can prevent a particular person from contacting you.

bullycide A very new legal term for suicide in which bullying is determined to be the primary cause.

child pornography Movies or images that depict sexually explicit activity involving a minor.

concision Saying what you mean clearly and by using as few words as possible.

cyberbullying Hostile interactions over cell phones, on message boards, in chat rooms, or through social networking sites, occurring between friends or acquaintances and targeting someone personally.

cyberstalking Continued harassment of a person through e-mails or instant messages.

emoticons Symbols of faces used in electronic communication to convey emotions such as happiness, sadness, anger, or surprise.

e-thugging Posturing toughness through Internet posts or text messages.

flame war A drawn-out argument between two or more people on the Internet, often drawing in people who were not initially involved and causing them to take sides.

flaming Hostile interaction over the Internet, on message boards, in chat rooms, or through social networking sites, generally between strangers.

Internet footprint The image of a person that can be gathered by the information about him or her available on the Internet, generally through search engines.

logical dump A process through which information is extracted from a cell phone.

physical dump A process through which the entire flash memory of a cell phone is copied.

privacy settings The settings on your profile on a social networking site that control who can see your posts, pictures, etc.

remote monitoring Software that connects a computer to another computer, allowing the monitoring computer to see all of the activity on the monitored computer, in real time.

sexting Exchanging sexually explicit text messages or pictures with another person through a cell phone.

texting The act of sending electronic text-only messages through a cellular phone.

trolling Frequenting Internet sites or chat rooms with the intention of starting arguments.

Canadian Centre for Child Protection/TELUS Mobile Safety
Web Site
615 Academy Road
Winnipeg, MB R3N OE7
Canada
(800) 532-9135
Web site: http://mobility.protectchildren.ca/app/en
The Canadian Centre for Child Protection provides education, prevention, and action surrounding all issues of child exploitation. This Web site provides information specifically regarding the safe use of cell phones.

Common Sense Media
650 Townsend, Suite 435
San Francisco, CA 94103
(415) 863-0600
Web site: http://www.commonsensemedia.org
This not-for-profit, nonpartisan organization is committed to helping kids and families make wise choices about the media to which they expose themselves and that which they create. The organization conducts research; reviews media such as movies, music, books, and video games; and provides resources for parents and teachers.

Internet Keep Safe Coalition

5220 36th Street North

Arlington, VA 22207

(703) 536-1637

Web site: http://www.ikeepsafe.org

This organization conducts research on global trends and
issues in the digital world, and it uses its findings to
develop products and resources for schools, educators, and
kids themselves to have safe Internet experiences.

i-safe

5900 Pasteur Court, Suite 100

Carlsbad, CA 92008

(760) 603-7911

Web site: http://www.i-safe.org

This organization is committed to educating and empowering
young people to create their own safe, responsible Internet
experiences. I-safe provides a K–12 curriculum, as well as
conducts community outreach to parents, law enforcement
officials, and community leaders.

National Crime Prevention Council

2001 Jefferson Davis Highway, Suite 901

Arlington, VA 22202-4801

(202) 466-6272

Web site: http://www.ncpc.org

This group provides information and resources about a vari-
ety of crime prevention topics, including cell phone
safety, Internet safety, and cyberbullying. It conducts

nationwide trainings and develops awareness programs that can be implemented in schools and community organizations.

NetSmartz Workshop
Charles B. Wang International
Children's Building
699 Prince Street
Alexandria, VA 22314-3175
(800) 843-5678
Web site: http://www.netsmartz.org
NetSmartz is a program of the National Center for Missing and Exploited Children. It provides interactive teaching resources such as videos, games, and activity cards to educate kids about digital safety. The Web site contains information, tips, and discussion starters about cell phones, cyberbullying, and more.

Sex Information and Education Council of Canada (SIECCAN)
850 Coxwell Avenue
Toronto, ON M4C 5R1
Canada
Web site: http://www.sieccan.org
SIECCAN provides information, resources, and services and conducts research in the area of sex education and sexual health, including issues of sexting and online exploitation.

Web Wise Kids
P.O. Box 27203

Santa Ana, CA 92799

(866) 932-9473

Web site: http://www.webwisekids.org

Web Wise Kids develops computer games that teach kids about Internet safety and prepare them to deal with issues like sexting, flaming, and cyberbullying. The organization also provides resources for parents and teachers.

Web Sites

Due to the changing nature of Internet links, Rosen Publishing has developed an online list of Web sites related to the subject of this book. This site is updated regularly. Please use this link to access the list:

http://www.rosenlinks.com/FAQ/Text

Aboujoaoude, Elias. *Virtually You: The Dangerous Powers of the E-Personality*. New York, NY: W. W. Norton, 2011.

Atelier, Olivia. *A Newbie's Guide to Social Media*. Webster's Digital Services, 2011.

Crystal, David. *Txtng: The Gr8 Db8*. New York, NY: Oxford University Press, 2009.

Edginton, Shawn M. *Read Between the Lines: A Humorous Guide to Texting with Simplicity and Style*. Dallas, TX: Brown Books, 2009.

Engdahl, Sylvia. *Teen Rights and Freedoms: Electronic Devices*. Farmington Hills, MI: Greenhaven Press, 2012.

Espejo, Roman. *Teen Rights and Freedoms: Social Networking*. Farmington Hills, MI: Greenhaven Press, 2011.

Joinson, Adam. *Oxford Handbook of Internet Psychology*. New York, NY: Oxford University Press, 2009.

Kiesbye, Stefan. *Cell Phones and Driving*. Farmington Hills, MI: Greenhaven Press, 2011.

Kiesbye, Stefan. *Sexting*. Farmington Hills, MI: Greenhaven Press, 2011.

Lane, Frederick. *Cybertraps For the Young*. Chicago, IL: NTI Upstream, 2011.

Michaels, Kai. *Life, Love and Texting: A Teenage Love Story*. Kindle Edition, 2011.

Obee, Jennifer. *Social Networking: The Ultimate Teen Guide.* Lanham, MD: Scarecrow Press, 2012.

Rosen, Larry D. *Rewired: Understanding the iGeneration and the Way They Learn.* New York, NY: Palgrave Macmillan, 2010.

Rozakis, Laurie E. *U Cn Spl Btr: Spelling Tips for Life Beyond Texting.* New York, NY: Citadel, 2009.

Scott, Jess C. *EyeLeash: A Blog Novel.* Kindle Edition, 2009.

Sechler, Jeff. *A Young Adult's Guide to Safety in the Digital Age.* Camp Hill, PA: Sunbury Press, 2010.

Solove, Daniel J. *Understanding Privacy.* Cambridge, MA: Harvard University Press, 2010.

Turkle, Sherry. *Alone Together: Why We Expect More from Technology and Less from Each Other.* New York, NY: Basic Books, 2011.

Brown, John Seely. "Growing Up Digital: The Web and a New Learning Ecology." *Change*, March/April 2000, pp. 10–20.

Carroll, Jamuna, ed. *America's Youth* (Opposing Viewpoints). Farmington Hills, MI: Gale Group, 2008.

Carroll, Jamuna, ed. *School Policies* (Opposing Viewpoint). Farmington Hills, MI: Gale Group, 2008.

Debucquoy-Dodley, Dominique. "New York Looks to 'Modernize' Cyber Bullying Laws." CNN.com, September 27, 2011. Retrieved February 6, 2012 (http://articles.cnn.com/2011-09-27/politics/politics _new-york-cyberbullying_1_cyberbullying-phoebe -prince-tyler-clementi/2?_s=PM:POLITICS).

Don'tDriveandText.org. "Driving While Texting Statistics/Information." Retrieved February 11, 2012 (http://www.dontdriveandtext.org/Statistics).

Eisenberger, Naomi L., Matthew D. Lieberman, and Kipling D. Williams. "Does Rejection Hurt? An Fmri Study of Social Exclusion." Sciencemag.org, October 2003. Retrieved February 14, 2011 (http://www.sciencemag .org/content/302/5643/290.full).

Kennedy, Helen. "Phoebe Prince, South Hadley High School's 'New Girl,' Driven to Suicide by Teenage Cyber Bullies." *New York Daily News*, March 29, 2010.

Retrieved February 6, 2012 (http://articles.nydailynews
.com/2010-03-29/news/27060348_1_facebook-town-hall
-meetings-school-library).

Lauinger, John, and Edgar Sandoval. "Kin of Deliveryman Left
Brain-Dead by Texting Driver Won't Pull Plug, Vows Suit."
New York Daily News, September 22, 2010. Retrieved
February 6, 2012 (http://articles.nydailynews.com/2010-09
-22/local/29441588_1_tian-sheng-lin-nechama-rothberger
-texting).

Mooij, Bram. "Data Extraction from a Physical Dump."
DFINews.com, September 29, 2010. Retrieved February 11,
2012 (http://www.dfinews.com/article/data-extraction
-physical-dump?page=0,0).

Parker, Ian. "The Story of a Suicide: Two College Roommates,
a Webcam, and a Tragedy." *New Yorker*, February 6, 2012.
Retrieved February 7, 2012 (http://www.newyorker.com
/reporting/2012/02/06/120206fa_fact_parker).

Richmond, Riva. "Sexting May Place Teens at Legal Risk."
New York Times, March 26, 2009. Retrieved February 15,
2012 (http://gadgetwise.blogs.nytimes.com/2009/03/26
/sexting-may-place-teens-at-legal-risk).

Smahel, David, and Kaveri Subrahmanyam. *Digital Youth: The
Role of Media in Development*. New York, NY: Springer, 2011.

Virgin Mobile. "About Safe Text." Retrieved February 11, 2012
(http://www.practisesafetext.com).

Index

About the Author

Rebecca T. Klein writes books for young adults, and she enjoys singing, cooking, and playing outside. She is currently working on a master's degree in English education. Klein grew up in Detroit and lives in Brooklyn.

Photo Credits

Cover © iStockphoto.com/AVAVA; pp. 5, 29 Monkey Business Images/Shutterstock.com; p. 7 Monkey Business Images/ Thinkstock; p. 9 Stephanie Frey/Shutterstock.com; p. 16 oliveromg/Shutterstock.com; p. 19 Maria Teijeiro/Photodisc/ Thinkstock; pp. 25, 37, 50 © AP Images; p. 28 PT Images/ Shutterstock.com; p. 33 Caroline Purser/Photographer's Choice/Getty Images; p. 35 Chicago Tribune/McClatchy-Tribune/Getty Images; p. 39 Miroslav Georgijevic/The Agency Collection/Getty Images; p. 43 Yellow Dog Productions/The Image Bank/Getty Images; p. 44 Image Source/Getty Images; p. 46 Yuri Arcurs/Shutterstock.com; p. 48 auremar/Shutterstock.com.

Designer: Evelyn Horovicz; Editor: Bethany Bryan; Photo Researcher: Karen Huang